HARNESSING CHATGPT

HARNESSING CHATGPT

Strategies for Entrepreneurs

BILL VINCENT

RWG Publishing

CONTENTS

CHAPTER 1

Introduction

The implications of this algorithmic innovation are not only technical. In the first half of 2021, anyone can spend a few bucks building a model that promises to generate human-like text and conversation. It is then a promising time for entrepreneurs. Executives often prioritize other initiatives due to their immediate business impact. ChatGPT requires a significant budget of computational resources. And any business decision-maker would be missing out on emancipatory and growth opportunities by not choosing or exploring this particular direction. The relative simplicity of its "training strategy" further opens up interesting paths for businesses of all sizes. Whether you are an early-career professional starting your first project or founder of a thriving venture capital-funded startup or established company, there is a great opportunity for you to harness the power of the language model. In this small guide, I present strategies for entrepreneurs to include conversational GPT into their businesses. And this is only the seed, every solid idea presented here might grow into a specialized business itself.

I work with many entrepreneurs, founders, and corporate decision-makers. We throw around terms like AI, ML in casual conversation because it has become a part of our daily life and business. We don't always realize that we're using these terms to group together a spectrum of capabilities, ranging from very hard math theorems to simple programmable workflows, to even simpler rule-based systems, and déjà vu-like experience (of conversational AI). This new notation, created a couple of years before my own birth, was named in the mid-nineties by our colleagues as GPT. In 2021, these four-keys models are powered inside beefy servers of OpenAI, breaking state-of-the-art records in practically every application of Natural Language processing. ChatGPT (previously known as DialoGPT) is a 10 billion parameter network, released during the COVID-19 pandemic for casual public use. Despite its size, this neural network executes in real-time or near-real-time, in cheap consumer devices, without even needing an internet connection. It was made possible to run all of its 1.3 teraflops in a single, common GPU, and the secret is pretty simple. 96% of its edges, or connections between computing nodes, do not need to be simulated while a large batch processes a large set of input examples. Instead, they can remain frozen, like a concrete street during sunny days.

CHAPTER 2

Understanding ChatGPT

In essence, the user is an autoregressive model for language modeling and generation. Given a prompt, an autoregressive model defines a probability distribution over the next token in a sequence. By iteratively sampling from this distribution and updating the prompt, the model can generate sequences of arbitrary length. Specifically, ChatGPT is an internal version of the generalized Prompt Tuning. Prompt tuning is a recent paradigm of "few-shot" fine-tuning that has been implemented on T5 and also proposed as a more generalized technique for other autoregressive-triggered architectures. It replaces the soft-token embeddings from the decoder attention, etc. In more detail, the authors propose to project prompt tokens via a non-linear projection-THEN activation (ELU), then multiply the inputs with the positional encoding to take structural information into account, then sum with the output of the prompt embeddings, then linear projection again to the token space dimension, and feed the output into the autoregressive generation (such as LSTM in the case of GPT) of the next word.

To test this product initially, I had the GPT-3, and now I am testing it using the GPT-3 implementation of OpenAI. I believe that learning how to use GPT-3 will help me use its version, ChatGPT, to increase my productivity in the business of my profession, which is the analysis of systemic intervention and coaching. Since 2020, I tried to have access to the user, but due to high demand, I did not receive a response. But currently, I am performing some research to understand the behavior of PTSD patients using natural language processing. Dr. Neissel, Ludmyla, informed me about ChatGPT, and currently, I am using it to develop some searches and work that require the user. I am enjoying this part of the work to maintain it and learn a little more about it.

2.1. What is ChatGPT?

GPT enabled machines to generate novel texts based on a given input paragraph. People have used GPT to generate narratives, write poems, generate captions, and much more. Typically, to use GPT-2 or GPT-3 based models, one needs to provide a "prompt" that describes the expected or required feature. The prompt can initially contain some initial or partial information regarding the feature. Once the chatbot knows the objective or expected feature, it uses its ability to predict outputs to generate text that meets the required features. Besides following the guideline, the GPT bot can occasionally introduce some randomness using the sampling strategy to mix text and avoid adding constrained outputs. During its training, the model is trained to avoid meaningless text. So, knowing the feature helps the bot only generate the meaningful feature. GPT's ability to generate is even more interesting. GPT-3, an iteration developed by OpenAI, is designed with 175 billion parameters.

Generation, prevention, and transformation (GPT) is a quite popular term among machine learning professionals. Essentially, GPT is an architecture that is popularized by using a big variant named GPT-2. GPT models are based on the Transformer architecture and have the ability to contextually combine the outputs from previous words (or pixels in a given input image's case) to generate outputs that are connected to those inputs contextually. This property makes GPT models interesting for a variety of natural language processing as well as sequence-based downstream tasks.

2.2. How does ChatGPT work?

In the fine-tuning pipeline, a dataset is typically reformulated into a sentence generation task, where we input both the conversation history and prompt into the ChatGPT model and force it to generate the next sentence. At this point, the weights in the ChatGPT model are fixed, and our own model learns by updating its own weights in order to minimize the losses between the generated sentence and actual response. Presently, there is not one universally agreed-upon metric for evaluating conversational models. However, many organizations look at perplexity and F1, as well as manual quality ratings of generated responses. Relatively speaking, these numbers are quite low compared to other more advanced methods, and the ChatGPT models are ranked at just 1-2. Overall, ChatGPT can work well, especially if the scale is produced to produce large-scale datasets. In fine-tuning, larger ChatGPT models better understand conversational contexts and better capture the nuances of a given dataset to generate responses more reflective of the provided training stimuli.

How does ChatGPT work? ChatGPT is a type of artificial neural network, which is essentially modeled after the human brain. It is constructed of small information processing units called artificial neurons, which are loosely analogous to the biological ones found in living systems. These are organized into three main types of artificial neurons: input neurons to receive input information, hidden neurons used for processing, and output neurons to produce some output. The input neurons take in an encoded representation of the input sequence, such as a sentence, paragraph, or longer document in the form of a real-valued vector, and a mathematical operation is used to classify or label that data. The neural network then processes the input data through a series of transformations until it arrives at the final layer, output neurons interpreting the processed information.

2.3. Benefits of using ChatGPT

3) 24/7 assistive service. Often, customers need support outside of standard business hours and do not have the flexibility to wait for customer service operations to open. They may need technical assistance or support from the company at times when these services would not typically be available outside of standard business hours. However, customer inquiries do not pause within these periods. Using ChatGPT, companies can help provide their clients with the information they need whenever they need it. This allows companies to assist them at any time or day of the week.

2) Scalable sales support. Many sales support calls involve helping customers find certain parts or difficult to identify or locate products. ChatGPT can help guide customers through searching for these items in order to minimize the time it takes to find the right product and purchase it. ChatGPT can answer questions like "what is this part called?" or "Can you show me what this particular item looks like?" As a result, sales support is easier to maintain and manage, and customers can receive products efficiently and quickly even when they are not able to call a representative for assistance.

1. Decreased customer service response time. Many companies use conversational AI tools to help customers find the information they need more quickly. Often a user is looking for simple and basic information and doesn't have the bandwidth to wait for a long time. ChatGPT can answer these questions

quickly and efficiently so that users can learn the information they need as soon as possible whenever they need it.

First, there are many benefits to using ChatGPT in a business, and many companies already use conversational AI to support their products and services. As we think about using ChatGPT, it's important to remember those benefits and think about how ChatGPT can help unlock powerful conversational AI capabilities. Some of these benefits include:

CHAPTER 3

Utilizing ChatGPT for Entrepreneurship

Reading through these possibilities could convince leaders that natural language models are best left to research with dedicated budgets but have little place in today's business market. These musings could be encouraging. Such questions encourage a review of modeling objectives and issues, both of which are important within our larger conceptual art and science boundary that is still in review today. As for possible environmental dangers, knowledge challenges capabilities to align solutions with Earth in a way that can dissipate suspicion. It's a smart idea.

By now, many people are aware of how convenient, collaborative, and satisfying it can be to interact with a conversational AI agent. The tech necessitates preparing for evolving customer expectations, of course. People should ordinarily be trained to manage these useful machines and to be alert to disruptions that could follow from rapid mass adoption. These machines depend on compute resources that generate significant increases in greenhouse gas production. Their work hinges upon quick, authoritative judgment about training data governance and representational choices. Without a real quantum leap in the underlying technology, it won't be easy to pivot when the weaknesses of the most recent systems are finally recognized and systematically attacked electronically. Even today, misinformation is widespread in social media and these natural language models are being set to work against societal norms and desires rather than in the service of them, further undermining democracy and the rule of law.

So, how can business leaders and entrepreneurs harness the power of a conversational AI model like ChatGPT, and should they? Josh from Fast knows what ChatGPT can do. He says, "ChatGPT, when in the hands of a skilled operator, is incredibly potent. We are making rapid and robust progress with it in solving our real-world self-service requirement. It's tough to beat getting our internal and external consumers what they require, whether it's support, education, or access to products, at scale, within quality expectations." When deciding whether and how to incorporate well-trained natural language models like ChatGPT into a company's capabilities, leaders can consider several perspectives.

3.1. Identifying use cases for ChatGPT

Which Frustrations Are Ready to Be Solved? This is an optimization problem: can you go through the users in a given customer segment and find an activity that takes a lot of their time and/or causes a lot of frustration while doing it? Often such activities could be resolved with a bit of variety, some productivity gains, or just some emotional support. A successful venture here goes through a subset of these activities and looks for high-value candidates from the trade-off triangle. A natural drawback of chat is that there's no graphical user interface which could additionally carry recommendations or clickable actions, but once the core chat components are in place, there's little downside to your model and its performance when introducing such idea-through-chat feature.

In this section, we'll provide you with a set of criteria to which you could map ideas in your head to quickly decide whether you want to take a given use case seriously - or spend your efforts elsewhere. This will be inspired by the coarse process used in chat-based AI startups to detect whether an idea is worth building further. The purpose of the initial exploration of your idea is not to get every one of your questions answered but to prevent you from "wasting time on something that doesn't add value for anyone". While this process is performed as a single call to zoom in on what you can actually expect out of the GPT-3 beta prompt API - not training - it should give you a rough idea of what you could (hypothetically) achieve by going larger scale with ChatGPT.

Modern language models, such as GPT-3, are demoed in a wide variety of use cases. But when entrepreneurs consider a novel language model like GPT-3, it might be less straightforward to answer the question: is my use case a good fit for this technology? Can I train a business that scales around it?

3.2. Integrating ChatGPT into customer support

ChatGPT offers the power of GPT-3 but, unlike OpenAI, it can and should be sold to several companies, not just one. The technology was developed at EleutherAI by people who really understand this type of software. So you can count on it and soon put in the hands of entrepreneurs around the world. In practice, you take what you can offer in the chatbot, set the price of the product going backwards determining what will be charged to the company. If this company is a good source of income for your pet project startup, you have a product that can make you money and the company will still have access to a chatbot without a name from the prestigious OpenAI.

Probably the first use of GPT-3 was in chatbots. These bots manage to hold good conversations and companies from several sectors have hired GPT-3 from OpenAI to help build their chatbots. However, OpenAI itself uses GPT-3 and the other versions of the software in other companies' chatbots and receives an undisclosed amount in return. What does that say? Not all entrepreneurs who want to create chatbots are willing to work with OpenAI. In addition, the amount of money requested by the company is not known and may be too high. There is also no information on the lead time for the implementation of the chatbot.

The dream of being able to speak to an AI system and work more naturally with it can finally become a real product. As we've already seen in this section, there is too much to learn, but still several opportunities already exist for entrepreneurs to explore ChatGPT and demonstrate that this technology is profitable.

3.3. Enhancing marketing strategies with ChatGPT

Only around 1.5% of all chats receive inquiries from visitors or clients. The software and Internet sector received approximately 18% of the chatbot orders. Throughout its peak growth in the Asia-Pacific (APAC) area, people in financial services established fifty percent of all chatbot requests. By 2020, worldwide IT and service would be worth USD 4.64 billion, with a current worth of USD 1.27 billion. The increased part of the solutions offered by the larger IT providers in this space will spark demand for smart financial technology. I do hope this clarifies the definition of chatbots, its functions, and innovative organization partnerships. As well as significant studies of the influence of chatbots across different sectors and entities, this study provides comprehensive understanding and knowledge of the current scenario.

Chatbots are invaluable for marketing strategies. They are especially useful when used to heighten user engagement. They can also be used as a 24/7 professional agent who communicates effectively. They can also advertise a future event and send reminders to attendees. A lot of firms have chatbots to educate, entertain, and joke with users. Nearly 40% of big companies have intent to fulfill and receive orders for chatbots as of 2016. Companies use chatbots to perform various tasks including both technical and functional inquiries. Some chatbots are created to execute and carry out orders from competitors. Chatbots are extremely useful in marketing. Conversational commerce comes with quick access and an efficient interface. Their main usage is from banking institutions. Live conversation increased by 45% between 2019 and 2020. Many individuals visiting a website are contacted by chatbots if the visitor is at risk. One may be asked to chat and begin to ask some inquiries by employees. In turn, bots and employees in digital finance have been able to effectively work with the messengers.

3.4. Leveraging ChatGPT for product development

We build an interface and a solution between ChatGPT and business, giving an idea for the feasibility and viability of a product. We build a model for investors and founders, with the help of a chatbot based on chat. ChatGPT to help you build your business model, can't say chat, product development. Provide conversational interfaces on software products, understand your business better. You can watch the video and the details of the implementation. We train ChatGPT, generate the conversation with possible questions involving project objectives, how the project aims to solve once brought to a chat bot. When I say it's, we have the scenarios and the added value in the solution. Understand the stages of the travel funneling, the right moment to use the chat by product of your business and conduct user interviews. This comes from a developed interface, validation and model of the created architecture. We automate the process and build a bot on the users.

Before you even start creating something, how do you know if it's going to be a hit or not? There are many signals a product can have that will make it successful, but perhaps the most important one is demand. If your product is a solution for an existing problem, you can bet on the first problem that intersects with the market needs. If you can create mapping of search trends before launches in the cases of product launches in large platforms, you have an idea of the viability of that product. Another solution, common in start-ups, is to create an MVP, Minimum Viable Product such that part of the functionality of the service that can already be used by users at the early stage. framework called GT Converter, chat version. GPT, today the work inserted to give us some guidance on this topic, centered on the application of text chat. A script using text chat is proposed for the market, which we have been reviewing the various opportunities to use in product development and special applications.

CHAPTER 4

Best Practices for Harnessing ChatGPT

The abstract idea becomes concrete when you look at what people are using ChatGPT for now. Accessibility is the first step. We ought to try the ChatBot Toys, then see how they help with open-ended queries people have about our products and services. You'll probably want to use a different kind of GPT to manage sensitive customer data but use a read-only access, supervised by the subject-matter experts to help your business close cases faster. But, for version one, I think the ChatGPT toys are a good start. Next is aspiration. You experiment with centaurs, where a ChatGPT agent can suggest a question that aligns with what the operator else had been typing. Finally, pro-action is the mountaintop. You let yourself get Google-mounted and are blown away by the profits.

How exactly can an entrepreneur benefit from these latest developments in conversational learning? It seems like an abstract concept. How exactly do you go from this "fine-tuning is transformational" to something that drives the business that entrepreneurs do? The idea that "chat GPT is transformational," once you've figured out what that means, has a vision-compelling impact. Moreover, only a few hands have actually driven the thing. So, it's abstract enough that a whole spaceship full of entrepreneurs might fixate on it and set forth on a 20-year journey to Mars, repeatedly cursing messages against a distant benefactor who lured them with a sweet siren of hope before disappearing over the horizon.

4.1. Training ChatGPT effectively

As the main focus of chatGPT is conversation generation, and we fine-tune the model towards conversational datasets, the preprocessing, tokenizing, and training process is pretty straightforward. After the initial, non-domain-specific training, you can start fine-tuning your GPT model. We usually do this based on big reddit data because it provides slightly more structured data than other conversational datasets built for AI training. As these datasets usually consist of a closed conversation between two modeling people doing API calls to the popular social platform, we need to recontextualize the responses in order for the training of our models to work. Therefore, we applied the commonly used trick of splitting the chatbot output data into fixed lengths, e.g. 150, making sure that the response is cut off by a whole sentence, making the chatbot learn to complete sentences as well as having an increased stability in the generation process.

One question one might be asking is "How do I need to train this GPT-3 model anyways?" There is no cookbook answer to this question because it depends on the initial setup of the GPT-2 model. The more conservative you train the model, the fewer hyperparameters you need and vice versa. Make sure to have enough data which is somewhat similar to the task you want to apply GPT-3 on. We trained chatGPT 2.0 with the option of training a language model, which worked flawlessly, and with a dataset of about 1.8 billion messages, but with a very large model with 1.7 billion parameters. Please note that if you are training your GPT model with a less extensive language model, it might have higher potential for fine-tuning, but then again, you risk overfitting your chatbot, as you can fine-tune more extensively with an overparameterized language model than with a more conservative model.

4.2. Ensuring ethical and responsible use of ChatGPT

Data ethics, or "fairness constraints," can provide information regarding biases in ChatGPT's outputs. Investments in research and creation of more diverse training data can also help address fairness concerns. Common sense and professional judgment can help fuel innovative solutions to these evolving questions. An example of misuse, for instance, we recently witnessed Earthly Search, a search engine that connects users to the climate change knowledge transfer network and brings them specific applications. If deployed irresponsibly, the platform could promote themes that are in tabs with the climate truth rather than seeing climate mitigation and adaptation efforts aimed at minimizing the impacts of climate change across the continent. Control and responsibility by developers can play a huge role in preventing misuse. With huge datasets that are used to train these models, how can we implement data ethics? First, don't use questionable data types - data that come with data ethics issues like racism, sexism, talking about hate speech, rules about exploitation of other people, animals, or the environment. Two, do not copy these unfair biases. Researchers like researchers must take a critical standpoint and raise questions about datasets and algorithms that mimic harmful systems. While complete ethical discussions about implementing systems or algorithms that mimic real-world effects can pose a challenge, the discussion must go beyond omitting clear negative actions.

Ensuring ethical and responsible use of ChatGPT and AI in general: Since these models have been trained on vast amounts of data from the internet, there is a lack of control over the types of content that these models generate. As a result, fake targeting of certain people or world events in distorting ways can occur. While there is no one-size-fits-all policy to establishing ethical guardrails for AI, startups using ChatGPT must weigh considerations such as privacy, bias, and misuse.

4.3. Handling potential challenges and limitations

Bias is a common feature of content generation models when they are trained on biased data. This model is likely to carry at least some of that bias into the text it outputs as well. Since it was trained on open source data, a more representative slice of human language than data that can be shared in a company context, my head model is likely less biased than a model trained on proprietary data. Even so, it is absolutely crucial not to build harmful applications based on these models or use the text output to lend authority to such applications. When building the system, it is essential to check the output and make sure that no harmful content is generated.

Chatbots based on large-scale language models are a double-edged sword. On one hand, chatbots that mimic human language can be very useful, and entrepreneurs are finding new and profitable applications for this technology. On the other hand, this type of chatbot can potentially be used to mislead and scam people, creating distrust toward AI systems. The last thing you want for your skillfully crafted start-up business is a trend that might let public opinion settle into something you are doing, but that you are not (or should not be) doing. There are several ways in which public perception could lead you into this unwanted category. It is your responsibility to think about these, and if possible, take preventative action.

CHAPTER 5

Case Studies: Successful ChatGPT Implementations

Arts and Culture. A ChatGPT implementation for the San Francisco Orchestra helped retain donors and answer audience questions about the upcoming events. Within a few weeks, the model learned to answer questions based on available data, structure offer information, and provide various donation options. While the solution didn't cover all provided functionality, it still worked well for known queries and significantly improved user engagement. The client was wowed by the capability of ChatGPT in rapidly producing results: a bit of data management and HTML formatting resulted in a $40k month-on-month increase in the donation amount.

Real Estate. A business in San Francisco's South Bay region is a member of a multiple listing exchange that features the best homes in the area. Viewings are by appointment for only a few days, with offers due a week after that, and often at the same time. They needed a chat solution that would help them communicate with interested buyers, answer questions about offer submission and house purchases, and schedule viewing appointments. To wit, they wanted the chatbot to be smart enough to find the right information in a back-end system irrespective of how many questions are asked or what context was previously established. In under two weeks, we were able to build and train a chatbot that rapidly became indispensable.

Here, we present examples across a variety of sectors to illustrate a wide range of potential ChatGPT uses.

5.1. Case Study 1: ChatGPT in e-commerce

Through the WhatsApp Commerce Help chat, Dukaan onboarded more than 2 lakh businesses in the lockdown. Many brands, influencers, and resellers began to adopt this feature as part of their e-commerce plan in the coming weeks. Dukaan helped Mom Store, a home furnishings brand, to alleviate the challenge of multiple payment requests and address consumers' questions about product features just before the selling season of Baisakhi started. Using Dukaan, the brand significantly improved its ease of sale and boosted gross merchandise value by 80% in comparison to the previous season. In the third wave of the pandemic, Lamaara, an online fashion boutique, saw an over 40% increase in orders, achieving 15% growth in the customer base. This brand split the Ghazal and semi-formal wear categories to meet product demand from its customers at the right time. The new strategy of increasing brand visibility and increasing customer orders was a result of Dukaan's assistance.

In the field of chatbots used by e-commerce companies, India's Dukaan could be a role model for many startups. The startup used various strategies to onboard many sellers through its instant messaging-based approach to directly recruit retailers via WhatsApp-based conversational chat. The main problem faced by Dukaan was to connect millions of small manufacturers and retailers with each other and then with the consumer by creating an easy-to-use platform. To address this issue, instead of creating a separate app for each manufacturer, it directed those manufacturers who did not have a website to promote their products to use Dukaan's WhatsApp Commerce Help application.

5.2. Case Study 2: ChatGPT in healthcare

The initial approach the company had in place was to generate canned responses related to patients' questions regarding medications, chronic illnesses, and any health-related subject. A doctor and a nurse comprised the team to be credited with generating tack responses. In both cases, these team members had been in the medical profession for at least 5 years. Should there be gaps in the GPT-3 response, this team could help refine the relevant informed replies. Either the response would show the capability of ChatGPT to display an adequate resolution, or there would be deficiencies that would rely heavily on the healthcare professional's contribution. Given these basic guidelines, the company engaged ChatGPT in a conversation.

In the healthcare domain, your team was working with a platform that enabled healthcare institutions to centralize and streamline their telemedicine and remote patient monitoring (RPM) services. In this other product, the company aimed to alleviate the financial challenges that arose for healthcare institutions when they went after their only sources of revenue (i.e., in-clinic care). However, these sources were somewhat derailed by the 2020 COVID-19 pandemic. The product included developing messaging components for patients and their care team members, such as clinicians and internal staff, in addition to allowing patients to conduct virtual visits. By offering RPM, the solution allowed caregivers to remotely monitor a variety of diseases as well as other medically relevant patient data, instead of providing in-person care. The goal was to provide both asynchronous and synchronous messages, in contrast to concurrent visits with their team members. The company's clients required a standalone application because most of them relied on paper-based services or unconnected applications/services. For the new solution, it was complex.

5.3. Case Study 3: ChatGPT in finance

In summary, ChatGPT can provide value to small entrepreneurs and large corporations alike, regardless of the amount of available data. Its versatility and ability to generate responses in natural language make it a useful tool in various practical scenarios.

For example, business owners in finance can leverage ChatGPT to interpret macroeconomic forecasts and make informed decisions. By using techniques like document summarization on financial reports or paragraph completion on language-specific company sentiment reports and financial instrument prices, smaller companies can gain insights and develop mitigation plans.

Data scarcity is a common challenge, even for experts in the field of AI. However, GPT-3 has been trained on a wide range of open domain data, enabling it to answer questions in different domains without requiring specialized training on more data. This makes it a valuable resource for resource-constrained companies.

ChatGPT is a versatile tool that can be utilized in various practical ways. It can benefit small entrepreneurs as well as large corporations, regardless of the amount of available data. Small to medium business owners who cannot afford expensive data platforms or have limited datasets can still find value in using ChatGPT.

CHAPTER 6

Future Trends and Innovations in ChatGPT

ChatGPT is also limited in that it is now less about the capacity of the AI agent and more about the information that it has stored. The training data may include noise, and verifying that data will take time. Making it easier to store information and obtain surveys, among other details, will increase the potential for misuse of AI systems. A preference for cheating based on a statistical model also exists retention check by allowing verification. To ensure you are on fire from the analytical investigation, you can be frustrated when chatting with AI. The data leaks things like discriminatory word supplementation in training data if the GPT model is trained on a variety of data sources drawn from the web. Other problems that are widely reported from temperature changes from improper natural language processing training have been contained in the estimate since its absolute release. Future improvements in GPT technology could alleviate or even entirely address the problems disclosed.

Letting an imagination-filled AI-based conversational assistant to interact with multiple applications inside an isolated context sounds cool. Another potential application of ChatGPT, which revolves around using virtual robots for venture creation. Startups might cost 10-100k USD right now, but by using a few agents in consultation with AI-based conversational assistants, it could take only a minute to define the project requirements. Many digital workers who have been employed in the venture phase will be cut off significantly. It can save between $5,000 and $200,000 during the period of two founders making ideas into products. An ecosystem of the entrepreneurial venture is possible. Alternatively, people create more elaborate startup rubber runs, and developers are contracted for complete sets of XP, preparing further birthday parties. Such startups are probably not viable.

6.1. Advancements in natural language processing

In the first four years of operation in the neural network, the most sworn metric has been the understanding of speech: the way it is used to evaluate its consistency. Ideally, proper understanding of the system should mimic the way humans think, evaluate information, and make decisions. Chatbots are a powerful conversational tool, and in a Deep Learning community, their effectiveness and intelligence are often measured by the results of the speech assessment metric. Unfortunately, ever since chatbots have been developed, significant challenges have been identified in terms of linguistics and semantics. This is due to the high rhetoric of unintentional learning skills, as described by original author Dhawen Vaswani in the famous attention and convolution mechanism, which has resulted in a transformational mode of neural network architecture.

In 2020, OpenAI released a curious chatbot called ChatGPT. It was the byproduct of many advances in natural language processing, which is the foundation of chatbot effectiveness. According to this metric, since 2010, progress had been incremental until late 2017, when machine performance began to exceed human performance in this task. What exactly happened in 2017 to boost machine performance suddenly? The answer is a clever neural network architecture. Before 2017, the most commonly used conversational engine was the one inside Siri, called SiriVoiceAssistant. Siri had to be trained by human speech transcriptions that were later used to drive its conversational capabilities through deep learning. However, ChatGPT's neural network architecture uses 'multiheaded self-attention' mechanisms, which focus more on the bits of the input sequence that are most important and need more weave inclusion in the output. The transformer-based neural architecture improved the effectiveness of the state-of-the-art conversational agent.

6.2. Integration of ChatGPT with other technologies

The current architecture would make accelerations in humanity's progress unprecedented with meaningful quality of life improvements. Technology could allow for more time for humans to better practice meditation, art, science, and sports. Practicing these activities make us better, stimulate creativity, and teach our minds positivity while broadening our perception of the world. There are other areas that could be even better improved, such as health, physical and mental well-being, consciousness, education, and wisdom. A 3000 IQ intellectual model could end humanity's suffering, foster cure development and other relevant breakthroughs, allocate effective ways to plan and execute most practical mockups which can validate theories and extreme concepts. It could teach us wellness optimization and well-being breakthroughs. The businesses that accomplish these developments first would cause enhanced positive environmental, psychological, cultural, social, personal, and cognitive consequences. This process could collapse industries while other businesses relying on these would prosper even more.

This architecture could go beyond Uncle Ben's verbal abilities. For tasks which it's not fit for, external resources and processes could be triggered so that these could feed or guide the model. Some automation procedures could be taken at the same time. When the process ends, all results could be given to that architecture. In other words, this specific architecture could outperform all of today's businesses and professions which require extensive knowledge from a near-human level. Other architectures could measure all efforts done by helping humans and processes so that management would be easier to visualize and simulate in order to drive final decisions. Think about an intelligent search algorithm using vast external data in your business' planning meetings for thousands of possible tips. Thence, your architecture could populate the environments, use some additional processes to trigger the strategy projects, and guide total profit by using several simulations with quantitative tips.

6.3. Potential impact on entrepreneurship

Generating product solutions for new markets. In the project management market, AI is being utilized to extract knowledge from organization data, predict success, create plans, run simulations, assign tasks, and make informed choices. However, sometimes start-ups want to innovate strategies and services such as creating next-generation software products that need the machine to produce many innovative product concepts for a market with spurious and unrestricted ideas of all kinds. According to 80% of managing partners in Silicon Valley, it is also useful to have the means to generate creative solutions for new opportunities, contending product offerings using AI, especially GPT-3. GPT-3's as an idea engine can help generate product and service ideas for startups in new markets to solicit serious feedback and support businesses attempting to scale more quickly into new regions.

Automating research and development. Over 37% of CTOs want fine-tuned chatbots to help with research and development. GPT-3 can quickly iterate ideas for brainstorming company resources for startups, which can lead to strategic insights based on the latest in proprietary domain-specific, unsupervised, or unstructured data.

Automating an iterative process. Increased customer engagement is often built on scalable and repeatable methods. Fine-tuned GPT-3 can quickly help identify effective language patterns and conversation starters for chatbots and AIs, allowing those initial findings to increase customer engagement and upsell opportunities.

Harnessing ChatGPT: Strategies for Entrepreneurs. In the entrepreneurial context, the suggested applications mentioned in this paper can be utilized with even more potential. Increasing customer engagement by incorporating chatbots into a company's website, creating opportunities for upselling, providing a recommendation engine to help increase sales, creating the capacity to provide 24/7 customer service, engaging in innovative strategies and services, and generating ideas for new services and products. Here are other ways to strategically utilize fine-tuned ChatGPT in an entrepreneurial context.

CHAPTER 7

Conclusion

Regardless of the mode, they will also begin to form the intellectual capital surrounding the business problems in their firms and create the building blocks for what we at OpenAI generally refer to as AI governance. In developing the roadmap to achieving the future OpenAI capabilities, we form the foundation that our future products and services are built upon. This enables us to maintain a cutting-edge AI capability and serve as a touchstone for the AI practitioner to serve the interests of their firm.

In a business context, executives and practitioners can start to plant the seeds of the future OpenAI capabilities within the operations of their firms. They can do this by exploring how to leverage OpenGPT 3 to solve their business problems. In doing so, they will find that solutions segregate into those that are best served in a reactive mode and those that are best served proactively.

The function of OpenAI shouldn't be solely about the end result. It should be serving as an organizational capability that's internalized and used in every aspect of your work.

Consider that with ChatGPT 3, you can now ask your computer for the information you need and then tell it to give you an example of how it can be understood. It's a bit like asking a teacher to explain something and then asking it to prove its understanding by giving examples. This was not generally possible with ChatGPT 2 and goes far beyond performing a simple question and answer function.

As you continue to experiment with ChatGPT, the most important thing is to get started. Next, test and learn. The suggestions outlined guide you in the right direction, but there is no one-size-fits-all solution. Given that you have access to OpenAI, don't think of it as just another tool. Your access to this new capability should fundamentally change how you think about what's possible with your products and services.

Milton Keynes UK
Ingram Content Group UK Ltd.
UKHW040329031224
452051UK00011B/316

9 798330 245741